GET
W.R.I.T.E.

Share Your Message and Become A Published Author

ROBERT L. WATTS, JR.

To:

____

Contents

an email away if you need my assistance to navigate through this. I will be honored to add you to my growing list, as I have helped many others fulfill their dreams of becoming published authors. May God's grace be with you on this journey.

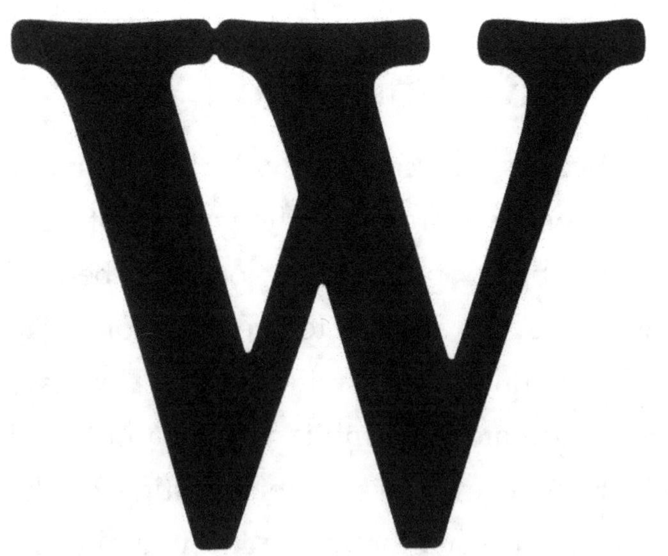

One

Why Should You Write

Let us commence with the primary interrogative pronoun, the genesis of how one's book publishing journey begins, which is the answer to the question, *why* would you want to write a book? There are approximately 2.2 million books published worldwide every year which testifies to the diverse reasons that drive individuals, like yourself, to take on this endeavor. Before delving further, I wish to impart some encouragement to anyone who are second-guessing themselves which resulted from contemplating the aforementioned statistic that many others are already publishing books.

Such adverse thoughts could lead one to question if their contribution(s) will be significant to our current cultural and literary history. However, this notion is far from true. Each author's work is unique and plays a vital role in enriching our collective literary heritage.

My initial motivation for writing was sparked by a challenge and inspiration from my daughter when she was around four or five years old. Allow me to share a delightful story about how it transpired. As a father, husband, ministry leader, worker president of our 501c3, and director of the growing education division of our 501c3, my schedule was already tightly packed. During the younger years of our daughter, she stayed at home with her mother before being enrolled in preschool. In 2010-11, she observed her mother's production of a children's book based on our daughter's fifth birthday celebration, "The Creative

Crayon Color Party." A very captivatingly written and beautifully illustrated book is beloved by all children who read it.

Our daughter is a creative individual who enjoys handcrafting gifts for us, especially for me, when I return home from work. Her bright, beaming face eagerly awaits my arrival, and she presents me with one of her heartfelt creations wrapped in colorful paper. As I unwrap her gifts, she exclaims her favorite phrase, "Open it, open it!" Who could resist such sweet innocence and charm? One day, while sitting at her little desk in her mother's office, she decided to make a book. She folded several sheets of 8.5 x 11 paper (landscape), drew crayon-colored images on them, and stapled the folded edges to create her masterpiece.

When I arrived home that day, I found her working industriously at her little desk alongside her mother. She informed me that she was making a book just like her mother. I was proud of her efforts and always cheered her on with whatever she chose to do. But then, she posed a profound question, "Dad, mom has her book, and I have my book," as she added the finishing touches with her crayon, "but where's your book?" For a brief moment, I was stumped by my little one's query.

I stood there, contemplating how to provide a reasonable answer as to why I had not attempted to write a book myself. I had not even considered the possibility until that moment. All I could say was something deflective, redirecting the attention back to her book, as we flipped through the pages of her hand-drawn pictures. However, that exchange stirred something within me.

Time passed, and in 2011, I co-authored a book with my wife for the married and engaged, "11:11, What Time Is It?" It was my first foray into writing and book publishing, and it sparked a love for the craft that has grown with each passing year. I have been known to express nuggets of wisdom in short, slogan-like statements, which a dear friend of ours would jokingly refer to as "a lot of nothingness." However, in all seriousness, she would encourage me to write a book as well.

As I previously mentioned, my schedule was quite hectic, and from my perspective, there was no time for me to draft a book. As you reflect on what others might have said to you or information you've had a fervent desire to share, can you begin to see what your 'why' you should write a book? I hope your answer is a strong, "YES!" Take a moment and write on the following lines why do you feel a book is of best interest:

____

____

____

Engaging in the short effective activity of drafting a clear and concise statement regarding the reasons behind one's inclination to pen a book serves as a catalyst for activating and stimulating one's emotions, ideas, and intentions towards becoming a published author. Frequently, individuals may express having authored numerous pages of written material, either handwritten or typed, throughout the course of their lives, but fail to progress beyond the classification of a "writer" until their works have been officially published.

As a writer and published author, I understand how one willingly provides readers with an unparalleled level of access into their lives. This access may manifest itself in the form of a biographical literary piece, or the sharing of information and knowledge. Furthermore, as an author, one grants readers a glimpse into their brand, creativity, and offers an unparalleled experience that allows readers to truly connect with the writer's vision.

The literary world, therefore, becomes a vessel through which authors can convey their messages to their readers, which will solidify the author's brand. Regardless of the genre in which an author chooses to operate, be it inspirational, suspenseful, romantic, or mysterious, there are legions of eager readers awaiting the literary exploration of the author's work.

As such, it is crucial to recognize that one's willingness to share a portion of themselves with the world is the first step towards authorial success, and should not be hindered by feelings of intimidation, for the author retains complete control over how they are perceived by their readers.

Writing is a powerful medium that allows individuals to express themselves, share their stories, and convey their ideas to the world. Becoming an author is a rewarding and fulfilling experience, as it allows you to communicate your unique perspective and contribute to the literary landscape. In this chapter, we will explore the reasons why one should become an author and share their story or learned information.

Writing is an incredibly therapeutic process that can help individuals to process their thoughts and emotions. By putting pen to paper, fingers to keyboard, or voice to text, authors can externalize their inner experiences and gain clarity on their own perspectives. Writing can be an outlet for creative expression, allowing authors to explore ideas, emotions, and experiences. It's a form of self-discovery and personal growth, allowing writers to reflect on their lives and the world around them.

Moreover, becoming an author allows individuals to share their stories and experiences with others. Writing can be a powerful tool for connecting with readers and creating empathy and understanding. By sharing their own experiences, authors can help others navigate similar situations and offer insight and guidance. Through your writing, authors can inspire, educate, and also entertain their readers, leaving a lasting impact on their lives.

In addition, writing is a form of legacy-building. By publishing their work, authors create a lasting record of their experiences, knowledge, and ideas. Writing is a way of leaving behind something meaningful for future generations, a testament to one's life and legacy. Through their writing, authors can make a lasting impact on the world, influencing the thoughts and ideas of generations to come.

Becoming an author can be a fulfilling and rewarding career. Writing can be a source of income, allowing authors to pursue their passion while earning a living. It's also a means of personal fulfillment, allowing individuals to pursue their creative passions and contribute to the world in a meaningful way. Becoming an author can be a journey of self-discovery and personal growth, leading to a sense of purpose and fulfillment.

Through writing, an author can process their thoughts and emotions, share their experiences with others, create a lasting legacy, and an ability to pursue a fulfilling career. Whether you are an aspiring writer or an experienced author, the act of writing can bring joy, meaning, and purpose to your life.

Authorship can be a journey of personal

growth. Writing require certain disciplines, perseverance, and willingness and courage to put yourself out there. The process of writing and publishing a book can teach you valuable life skills and lessons, such as time management, how to be a problem-solver, and effective communication. It will be a way to give yourself the needed challenge, stepping outside of your comfort zone, and taking the needed risks while you still pursue personal goals to attain.

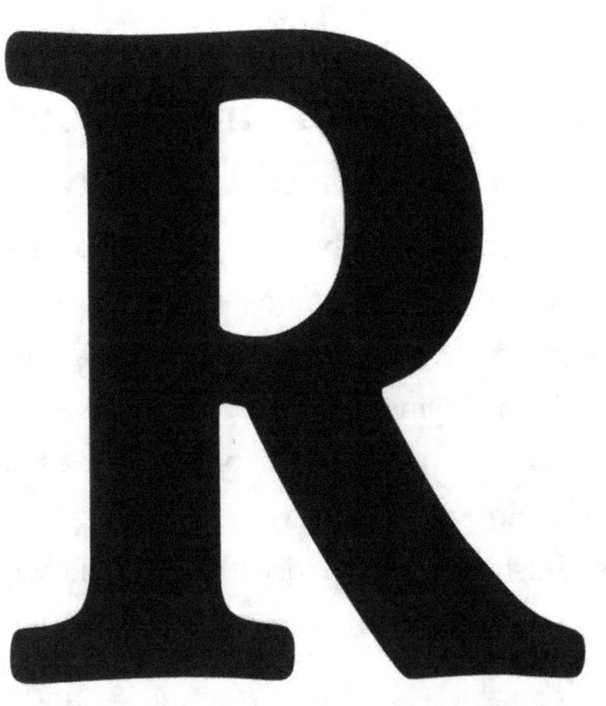

Two

Recognition and Record of Your Publication

Becoming a published author can be a powerful tool for establishing yourself as a subject matter expert in your field. Whether you're a business owner, an academic, or an industry professional, publishing a book can help you build your reputation and establish your expertise. In the following paragraphs will share reasons why.

Authoring a book gives you credibility in your field. It shows that you have a deep understanding of the subject matter and that you have taken the time to do the research and organize your thoughts in a meaningful way. Readers will be more likely to take you seriously and view you as an expert.

Also, when you publish a book, you have the opportunity to reach a wider audience than you may have otherwise. Your book(s) can be sold in bookstores or online, and shelved in libraries, giving you exposure to potential readers around the world. Additionally, publishing a book can lead one to media coverage, speaking engagements, and other opportunities that can help you further establish your expertise.

Authority is another attribute when writing a book. It gives you the authority to speak on a particular topic. When you're a published author, people will look to you for insights and guidance. You'll be seen as an expert in your field, which can lead to additional opportunities for sharing your knowledge and expertise.

The reach that comes with publishing a book can also help you expand your network. You'll have the opportunity to connect with other authors, publishers, and industry professionals who can help you further establish your expertise. You may even be approached for collaborations or speaking opportunities that can help you reach even more people in and out of your field, depending on your subject matter.

Being a published author can open up a world of opportunities for you. The exciting thought of chances to be invited to speak at conferences, write for publications, or participate in other industry events, is a great motivator. You'll also be able to further build your reputation as a thought leader.

A published author can be a valuable tool for establishing yourself as a subject matter expert. It can give you instant credibility, exposure, authority, networking opportunities, and increased opportunities to share your knowledge and expertise. If you're looking to establish yourself as an expert in your field, publishing a book can be an excellent way to do so.

Authors can be recognized as experts in their respective fields if their books are well-written, well-researched, and provide valuable insights into a particular subject. When an author publishes a book, they share their knowledge and expertise with the world. If the book is well-received and gain a wide readership, it can reiterate the author as a SME (Subject Matter Expert).

While not the only reason to write, there are also financial benefits to being an author. If your book is successful, you can earn a substantial income from royalties, speaking engagements, and other related opportunities. Even if you do not become a bestseller, writing is still an opportunity for a career choice, with freelance writing opportunities available in today's digital age.

An author's book can remain in public record indefinitely, depending on various factors such as the popularity of the book, the impact it has on readers, and its historical significance. Once a book is published, it becomes a part of the public record and is subject to copyright laws that protect the author's rights to their work.

The copyright protection last for the author's lifetime plus 70 years, in the United States. This means that during that time, the author's book will remain on the public record, and anyone who wishes to use the book or excerpts from it will need to obtain permission from the author or their estate.

Additionally, books can be archived in libraries and digital archives, ensuring their continued presence in the public record.

Libraries and archives play a crucial role in preserving the works of authors, while making the written published works accessible to future generations, like we currently enjoy and learn from the literary works of authors of old.

Books remain in the public record indefinitely, thanks to copyright protection and the archiving efforts of libraries and digital archives. As long as people continue to read and value the book, it will remain relevant and available to the public. Let's keep the legacy of authorship for many generations to come.

Three

The Inspiration, Influence, and Intellect as an Author

Authorship gives you the incredible power to inspire your readers in ways that can change their lives forever. When you write a book, you have the ability to take readers on a journey, to show them new worlds, to introduce them to fascinating characters, and to teach them new things. And in doing so, you have the power to inspire them to think, to dream, to learn, and to grow. Isn't it such an awesome responsibility given when becoming an author?

One of the greatest things about being an author is the ability to inspire readers to take action. Whether it's taking up a new hobby, pursuing a long-held dream, or simply looking at the world in a different way, your words can have a profound impact on the lives of those who read them. When readers connect with your message and find inspiration in your words, they can be moved to make positive changes in their lives. Grab a mirror of your phone and look at yourself. Tell yourself, "YOU, get to influence many through your book(s).

But inspiration is more than just a fleeting feeling. It's a powerful force that can motivate readers to take action, to pursue their dreams, and to achieve their goals. As a published writer author, you have the opportunity to inspire your readers to be their best selves and to reach for the moon. Your words can ignite them with the courage and the confidence they need to take necessary risks, to face challenges, and to overcome obstacles.

Through your writing, you can inspire readers to believe in themselves, to see their own potential, and to pursue their passions. You can offer them a sense of hope and a vision of what is possible. You can show them that even in challenging times, there is always a way forward. Giving hope through your words is powerful.

You will also have the power to inspire readers' demographics. Whether you're writing for children, young adults, or adults, your words can touch the hearts and minds of your readers, leaving them feeling uplifted, motivated, entertained, and inspired.

You are doing more than just writing and publishing books. You are making history and being a huge influence on the current and generations to come. When you write with passion and purpose, you have the ability to create a ripple effect of positive change that can touch the lives of countless people. So keep writing, keep inspiring, and keep changing the world, one reader at a time.

Although there's similarity between inspiration and influence, there are still set distinctions that influence as an author has on its readers. The influence of authorship on readers can be significant. Readers often associate a particular author with a certain writing style, genre, or subject matter, which can impact their decision to read a particular book or article. An author's reputation can also influence a reader's perception and their expectations for the quality and content of the writing. Such as Stephen King, we expect horror stories.

Readers may also be influenced by the author's background, experiences, and perspective. For example, readers may be more likely to trust the opinions or insights of an author who has relevant expertise or experience in the subject matter of the work. Conversely, readers may be less likely to trust an author who has a history of controversial or divisive statements or actions, unless the reader themselves can relate to it.

Overall, authorship plays a significant role in shaping a reader's perception of a particular work. It can influence their decision to read, trust, and engage with writing. Always recognize the power of your influence and don't take advantage of the platform.

Authors should not be in the habit of disregarding their influence on readers. As an author, it is important to be aware of the potential impact that your writing can have on others, and to take responsibility for the messages and ideas you're communicating. Don't take the cop-out approach of making it solely the reader's responsibility.

While it is ultimately up to readers to interpret and respond to your writing in their own way, as an author, you have a certain level of control over the content and tone of your work. It is important to consider how your words may be received by different audiences, and to strive to create work that is thoughtful, respectful, and reflective of your values and beliefs.

At the same time, it is also important to recognize that not everyone will agree with or appreciate your writing, and that it is impossible to please everyone. As an author, you should be prepared to receive both positive and negative feedback, and to respond to criticism with an open mind and a willingness to learn and grow.

Ultimately, by taking your influence on readers seriously, striving to create work that is both engaging and responsible, you can build a strong and loyal readership, and make a positive impact on the world through your writing.

As an author, the act of writing is not only a means of expressing oneself but also a way of informing and educating readers. By sharing our thoughts, experiences, and knowledge, we create a connection with our readers and help them gain new insights into various topics.

Realize that being an author helps inform readers by providing them with access to information that they may not have otherwise encountered. Whether it be through non-fiction writing, memoirs, or even fiction novels that incorporate historical events, authors have the ability to share their understanding of the world with readers. By doing so, readers are exposed to new perspectives and ideas that they can incorporate into their own thinking and decision-making.

Authors also have the power to educate readers by presenting complex ideas and concepts in a way that is accessible and easy to understand. By breaking down complex topics into digestible chunks, authors can help readers gain a better understanding of topics that may have previously seemed daunting. Whether it be explaining scientific concepts or delving into philosophical ideas, authors can make these topics more approachable and relatable.

Furthermore, authors can help inform readers by shedding light on important social issues and topics. Through their writing, authors can explore topics such as race, politics, social norms, gender, and much more, bringing awareness to issues that may have previously been ignored or overlooked. Through sharing their own experiences or perspectives on these topics, authors can spark important conversations and contribute to positive social change.

Being an author also allows us to inspire and motivate readers. By sharing our own stories of triumphs and struggles, we can help readers navigate their own challenges, find strength, and encourage them to persevere. Your published autobiographies or a self-help book, authors can provide readers with the tools and resources they need to achieve their goals and improve their lives.

Authoring books helps inform readers by allowing us to connect with them on a personal level. Through our writing, we can create characters and stories that resonate with readers, helping them to feel understood and less alone in their own experiences. This connection can be especially powerful for readers who may be going through a difficult time or struggling with mental health issues.

A published writer has a powerful tool for informing readers. Through writing, we can share our knowledge, educate readers, and spark important conversations about social issues. We can also inspire, motivate readers, and provide them with the tools and resources they need to achieve their goals and improve their lives. Ultimately, being an author allows us to connect with readers on a personalized level and create meaningful change in the world.

Authorship can be a strong indicator of intellect because it require a significant amount of mental effort and cognitive skills to produce a well-written book or piece of literature. Book writing involves numerous cognitive processes, including critical thinking, analysis, problem-solving, and creativity. These processes require an important level of intellectual engagement and a broad range of knowledge, which is reflected in the final product.

In addition, writing requires a strong language skillset, including a proficiency in grammar, syntax, and vocabulary. Authors must aim to have a deep understanding of language and the ability to use it effectively to convey their ideas and emotions. This requires a significant amount of intellect capacity, as well as an understanding of how language can be used to evoke different emotions and reactions in readers.

Four

A Trusted Source and Tell Your Story

In today's world of fake news and misinformation, being trustworthy is an essential quality for any author to possess. Becoming a trusted source means that readers can rely on your writing to be accurate, reliable, and unbiased. But, how do authors earn this trust, and what steps can they take to maintain it? Let's dive in.

Establish Your Expertise

Authors can establish themselves as experts in their field. This means staying up-to-date with the latest research, news, and trends in their niche. It also means building a body of work that demonstrates their knowledge and understanding of the subject matter.

One way to do this is to publish articles, essays, or books that showcase your expertise. By consistently producing high-quality content, you'll build a reputation as a knowledgeable and credible source. You may also consider offering consulting services and speaking engagements to further establish your authority.

Be Transparent and Honest

Transparency and honesty are key to building trust with your readers. Be clear about your sources of information and avoid any conflicts of interest that may compromise your integrity. This may include disclosing any of the financial or personal relationships that could have a direct effect of your work.

It's also important to acknowledge and

correct any mistakes or inaccuracies in your writing. Nobody is perfect, and admitting your errors shows that you take your work seriously and are committed to accuracy.

Engage with Your Readers

Engaging with your readers is another important aspect of building trust. Respond to comments and questions on your publications, social media accounts, and encourage feedback and dialogue. This not only shows that you value your readers' opinions but also allows you to address any concerns or misconceptions that may arise.

Engagement can also help you stay connected to your readers and understand their needs better. This, in turn, can help you tailor your content to meet their interests and expectations.

Maintain Consistency

Consistency is crucial in building trust as an author. This means delivering high-quality content regularly and maintaining a consistent voice and style. Readers are more apt to have trust in an author who consistently delivers reliable and insightful content. Consistency also extends to your online presence. Ensure that your website, social media accounts, and other online profiles are up-to-date, professional, and aligned with your brand and message.

Cultivate a Strong Network

Finally, cultivating a strong network can help you establish yourself as a trusted source. This means building relationships with experts, journalists, and influencers in your field. By connecting with others, you can gain insights, expand your reach, and collaborate on projects that can boost your credibility.

Networking can also help you stay on top of industry news and trends, which can further enhance your expertise and reputation.

As a trusted source, an author requires the combination of expertise, transparency, engagement, consistency, and networking. Through following these principles, you can establish yourself as a reliable and credible source of information and earn the trust of your readers.

Publishing a book can be a powerful way to share your story and connect with others. When you write a book, you have the opportunity to express your ideas and experiences in a way that can resonate with readers and help them understand your perspective.

Through your book, you can share your unique voice, insights, and experiences with the world, and in doing so, you can potentially inspire, educate, or entertain others. Whether you are writing a memoir, a novel, or a nonfiction book, the act of putting your thoughts and feelings into words can be cathartic and transformative.

In addition, publishing a book can also help you establish yourself as an expert in your field or as a thought leader in your community. It can open doors to new opportunities and help you connect with like-minded individuals who share your interests and passions.

Of course, writing a book can be a challenging and time-consuming process, and it may require a significant amount of dedication and perseverance. However, if you have a story that you are passionate about sharing, the rewards can be well worth the effort.

As an individual, you possess a unique story to share. Your experiences and perspectives are unparalleled, making it imperative that you take ownership of your voice. Transparent sharing is one of the most effective ways to connect with others, and writing about your compelling or humorous narrations can provide to be a valuable source for readers. By publishing your work, you can transcend the confines of your immediate audience, extending the reach of your message and potentially providing an opportunity for others to learn and grown from your experiences. Embrace the prospect of being a positive influence, so share and consider authoring.

Five

Empower, Entertain, and Empty

What an empowering experience it is as an author. Writing is a powerful tool that allows individuals to express themselves, share their ideas, and make an impact on the world. Whether it's through novels, short stories, poetry, or non-fiction works, being an author can give people a sense of purpose, confidence, and agency.

One of the primary ways in which being an author empowers people is through the act of creation. Writing allows individuals to create something entirely new, bringing their ideas and visions to life. This can be an incredibly fulfilling experience, giving authors a sense of accomplishment and pride in their work.

In addition to creating something new, being an author also empowers people by giving them a platform to share their ideas and perspectives with the world. Writing gives the ability to authors to communicate their thoughts, beliefs, and values in a way that can be easily understood by others. It is a powerful usage for marginalized or underrepresented groups, as writing can provide a means of amplifying their voices and advocating for change. The power of the pen is in the author's hand.

Empowering readers as an author can also encourage individuals to take control of their own narratives. Writing provides a space for people to explore their identities, experiences, and emotions, and to tell their stories in their own words. This can be especially important for individuals who feel silenced or marginalized by societal norms or expectations.

In addition to personal empowerment, being an author can also have broader societal impacts. Writing can inspire and inform others, encouraging them to think critically about the world around them and to take action for positive change. Whether it's through fiction that raises awareness about social issues or non-fiction that provides a roadmap for activism, writing can have a transformative impact on individuals and communities alike.

Of course, being an author is not always easy. Writing can be a challenging and sometimes isolating experience, and there may be setbacks and disappointments along the way. However, for those who are committed to their craft, being an author can be an incredibly rewarding and empowering journey.

In conclusion, being an author can be a

powerful and transformative experience. Through the act of creation, the sharing of ideas, and the ability to control one's own narrative, writing can empower individuals to make a difference in their own lives and in the world around them. Whether it's through personal fulfillment, social change, or broader cultural impact, authoring can provide a sense of purpose and meaning that is truly empowering.

One of the primary functions of authorship is to entertain readers. Fiction, in particular, has the power to transport readers to new worlds, introduce them to compelling characters, and tell engaging stories that keep them hooked from beginning to end. But how exactly does authorship achieve this?

One way that authorship entertains readers is through the use of storytelling techniques. A well-written story has a clear plot that is engaging and suspenseful, with enough twists and turns to keep the reader interested. The characters should be well-developed, with distinct personalities and motivations that make them relatable and interesting. Additionally, the setting and atmosphere of the story should be vividly described, transporting the reader to a different time or place, and immersing them in the story.

Another way that authorship entertains readers is through the use of language. A skilled author can use language to evoke emotion, create levels of tension, and build suspense. Using metaphors, similes, and other literary devices that enhances the language, makes it more engaging. The use of dialogue can also make the story more interesting, as readers get to know the characters through their interactive words.

Another perspective shows storytelling and language, authorship can also entertain readers by providing them with a sense of a mental retreat. Reading a book can be a form of relaxation, allowing readers to immerse themselves in a story and forget about their problems for a while. This can be especially important in times of stress or anxiety, as books can provide a much-needed respite from the real world.

Your authorship will entertain readers and provide them with a sense of a connected community. Readers who enjoy the same books or authors can connect with each other online or in person, sharing their thoughts and opinions about the stories they love. This sense of community can be especially important for people who feel isolated or disconnected from others in their daily lives.

Additionally, authorship can provide readers with a sense of community and connection, creating a shared experience that can be enjoyed by people from all walks of life. Whether it's through a thrilling mystery, a heartwarming romance, or a thought-provoking work of literary fiction, authorship has the power to entertain and delight readers of all ages and backgrounds. It is such an incredibly entertaining experience for readers when authors utilize storytelling techniques, language, and a sense of escape, and keep them engaged from beginning to end.

Emptying yourself in your writing can be a powerful, liberating experience. It's about shedding preconceived notions, letting go of inhibitions, and tapping into your innermost thoughts and emotions to create with abundance. Emptying yourself allows you to access your deepest creativity and authenticity, and it can lead to the most impactful and meaningful writing.

One of the first steps in the journey of emptying yourself as an author is letting go of expectations. This includes expectations about what your writing should be, how it should be received, and how it should compare to others. When you release these expectations, you free yourself from self-doubt and judgment, and you create space for your unique voice and perspective to emerge. This is the foundation for authentic and powerful writing.

Emptying yourself also means letting go of fear. Fear of failure, fear of criticism, fear of not being good enough - these are common fears that can hold authors back from fully expressing themselves. But when you embrace vulnerability and courageously face these fears, you open yourself up to new possibilities and opportunities for growth. Embracing fear as a natural part of the creative process allows you to write without constraints and inhibitions, and it is an enriching path to breakthroughs in your writing.

Another essential aspect of emptying yourself as an author is being present in the moment. This means you have to let go of distractions, silencing the inner critic, and fully immersing yourself in your writing. When you are present, you are able to tap into your intuition and connect with your innermost thoughts and emotions. You are able to write from a place of authenticity and truth, and your words carry a depth and resonance that can captivate readers.

Emptying yourself also involves being open and receptive to inspiration from various sources. This includes being curious, exploring innovative ideas, and being willing to take risks in your writing. It means being open to feedback and constructive criticism and being willing to revise and refine your work. When you are open, you allow yourself to be guided by the flow of creativity, and you invite new perspectives and insights into your writing.

In addition to letting go and being open, emptying yourself also requires self-care and self-compassion. Writing can be an emotionally and mentally taxing process, and it's important to take care of yourself along the way. This includes practicing self-compassion by way of treating yourself with kindness and understanding and acknowledging that writing is a journey with ups and downs. It also means taking breaks when needed, engaging in activities that nourish your mind and body, and maintaining a healthy work-life balance.

Emptying yourself as an author is not about depleting yourself, instead, it's the ability to tap into an abundant source of creativity within you. It's about creating from a place of abundance, where ideas flow freely, and you are connected to your innermost thoughts and emotions. It's about trusting in your own unique voice and perspective and allowing your writing to be an authentic expression of who you are.

Final thought on emptying yourself, as a

published author there's a powerful and transformative process. It involves letting go of expectations and fear, being present in the moment, being open to inspiration, and practicing self-care and compassion. When you empty yourself, you create space for your authentic voice to emerge, and you tap into an abundant source of creativity within you. Embracing this process can lead to profound and impactful writing that resonates with readers and leaves a lasting impact. So, let go, be present, and embrace the art of emptying yourself as an author for a truly transformative writing experience.

LET THE WRITING BEGIN

Six

Clearing the Mental Clutter

Now that you've read through some of the reasons to write and publish your book, it's time to start with the actual steps on how to do so. Please note that the following pages are some suggested steps based on personal experiences and any information gleaned from other authors. But it is not to be taken as the only method of doing so.

Writing a book is a complex and creative endeavor that requires careful organization of your thoughts to bring your ideas to life. Before you start putting pen to paper or fingers to keyboard, taking the time to get your mental thoughts together can greatly enhance your writing process and improve the quality of your book. Here are some key tips for clearing the mental clutter and organizing your thoughts before writing your book.

Reflect and Plan: Start by taking some time to reflect on your book's concept, theme, and purpose. What do you want to convey to your readers? What message do you want to share? Consider the main ideas, key points, and overall structure of your book. Create a plan or outline that outlines the main sections or chapters of your book, and the key ideas or topics you want to cover in each section.

Clear Your Mind: Before you start writing, take some time to clear your mind and create a conducive mental space for writing. Practice relaxation techniques, such as deep breathing or meditation, to calm your mind and focus your attention.

Clear away any distractions, and create a writing atmosphere that provide you with concentration and creativity. This can help you approach your writing with a clear and focused mind, ready to bring your organized thoughts to life on the page.

Brainstorm and Free Write: Once you have a general plan, allow yourself to freely brainstorm and jot down any ideas, thoughts, or insights that come to mind. Don't worry about organizing them at this stage - just let your creativity flow and capture your thoughts without judgment. This can help you get your ideas out of your head and onto paper and create a starting point for organizing your thoughts later.

Categorize and Prioritize: After you have generated a list of ideas, thoughts, and insights, review them and categorize them into relevant topics or themes. This can help you see the common threads and connections between your ideas and identify any gaps or overlaps. Prioritize your ideas based on their relevance and importance to your book's concept and purpose. This can help you create a clear framework for organizing your thoughts.

Create an Outline: Once you have categorized and prioritized your ideas, use them to create a detailed outline for your book. Start with a high-level outline that includes the main sections or chapters of your book, and then break down each section or chapter into sub-topics or sub-sections. Use bullet points or numbered lists to organize your thoughts in a logical and coherent manner. This outline will serve as a roadmap for your writing and help you stay focused and organized as you progress.

Review and Revise: After creating your outline, take the time to review and revise it. Ensure that the flow of ideas is logical and coherent, and that the structure of your book makes sense. Make any necessary adjustments or additions to ensure that your thoughts are well-organized and aligned with your book's concept and purpose. This review and revision process can help you refine your ideas and set a solid foundation for your writing.

Organizing your thoughts before writing your book is a critical step in the writing process. By reflecting, planning, brainstorming, categorizing, outlining, and clearing your mind, you can create a solid foundation for your writing and enhance your ability to communicate your ideas effectively to your readers. Taking the time to get your mental thoughts together can streamline your writing process, improve the coherence of your book, and ultimately result in a more impactful and well-structured piece of writing.

Say this out loud: "Excuses are abuses to my future." Don't let you get in your way from accomplishing the goal of publishing your book. Eliminating excuses and taking action to write a book can be achieved through disciplined approaches and your commitment to the process of writing. Following a few suggested strategies that can help you eliminate excuses and make progress towards completing your book.

Possibly start by setting a target word count for the writing session or completing a certain number of chapters by a particular deadline. Break down your writing goals into smaller, manageable tasks, and create a writing schedule that aligns with your other commitments. With a clear plan and timeline, you can hold yourself accountable and reduce the chances of making excuses to avoid writing.

Develop a writing environment that is conducive for productivity. Minimizing distractions and optimizing your writing space is a requirement. Find a quiet or with music and comfortable place to write where you can focus without interruptions. Turn off notifications on your electronic devices, close unnecessary tabs on your computer, and set aside dedicated time for writing without multitasking. Having a designated writing space and minimizing distractions can help you stay focused and productive, reducing the temptation to make excuses and procrastinate.

Cultivate a writing routine and mindset: Establishing a consistent writing routine and cultivating a positive writing mindset can help you stay motivated and disciplined. Make writing a regular habit by setting aside dedicated time for writing each day or week. You must approach it like a professional commitment and prioritize it in your schedule-WITH NO EXCUSES. Adopt a positive perspective towards writing by acknowledging that it is a process that will require effort and dedication. Embrace the imperfections of early drafts and allow yourself to write freely without self-judgment. Remember that progress is more important than perfection, and every writing session brings you closer to completing your book.

By setting clear goals, creating a conducive writing environment, and cultivating a consistent writing routine and mindset, you can eliminate excuses and make considerable progress towards completing your book. Stay committed to your writing process, be accountable to yourself, and pushing forward despite challenges or setbacks. Remember that writing a book is a labor of love. Be tenacious. Persevere. Be relentless until your book comes to fruition.

Seven

Developing Your Story

When it comes to writing a book, one of the most critical steps is developing your story. This process involves crafting a compelling and engaging narrative that captivates readers from beginning to end. Here are some key tips to help you develop your story effectively, especially for fiction:

Start with a Solid Idea: Every book begins with an idea. It could be a concept, a theme, or a character that inspires you. Take the time to brainstorm and generate multiple ideas. Consider their potential for conflict, tension, and emotional resonance. Choose an idea that excites you and has the potential to resonate with readers.

Outline Your Plot: Once you have a clear idea, outline your plot. Create a roadmap of the story, including the main events, conflicts, and resolution. Outline the beginning, middle, and end of your story, and ensure that there is a clear and compelling structure that keeps readers engaged.

Develop Your Characters: Characters are the heart of any story. Take the time to flesh out your main characters, including their backstory, motivations, strengths, weaknesses, and desires. Create well-rounded and relatable characters that readers can root for or empathize with.

Build Conflict and Tension: Conflict and tension are the driving forces behind a compelling story. Introduce obstacles, challenges, and conflicts that create tension and propel the story forward. Consider external conflicts such as obstacles and antagonists, as well as internal conflicts such as inner struggles and emotional dilemmas.

You must *Show Us, Don't Just Tell Us*: Use descriptive language and sensory details to bring your story to life. Instead of telling readers what's happening, show it through actions, dialogue, and vivid descriptions. Use all five senses to create a rich and immersive reading experience for your readers. Utilizing a thesaurus or online tools to find alternative words is also helpful.

Edit and Revise: Writing is a process, and your story may evolve as you progress. Be prepared to revise and edit your story to refine your plot, characters, and writing style. Seek feedback from beta readers or writing groups to gain valuable insights and make necessary changes.

Stay True to Your Voice: Stay true to your unique voice as a writer. Write from the heart and infuse your story with your own flavor, personality, emotions, and perspective. Authenticity and originality is what will make your story stand out and resonate with readers.

Reiterating that the development of your story is a very crucial step in the book writing process. It involves starting with a solid idea, outlining your plot, developing your characters, building conflict and tension, showing rather than telling, editing and revising, and staying true to your voice. By following these tips, you'll be on your way to creating a compelling and engaging story that will captivate readers and leave a lasting impact.

Eight

Embracing Your Work

Confidence in your work allows you to share your story with the world and connect with readers on a deeper level. Here are tips on how to be confident in what you wrote as an author. Embrace Your Unique Voice: Your writing style is what sets you apart as an author. Embrace your unique voice and writing style and be proud of it. Don't compare yourself to others or try to mimic someone else's style. Be confident in your own voice and trust that it will resonate with your readers who appreciate your authenticity.

Believe in Your Story: You spent time and effort crafting your story, so believe in it. Have faith in the story you are telling and the message you are conveying. Trust your storytelling skills and the choices you made in your writing. Remember that you are the creator of your story, and your perspective is valuable.

<u>Embrace</u> Feedback: Feedback is an essential part of the writing process. Be open to receiving feedback from beta readers, editors, or critics, and partners. Embrace constructive criticism as an opportunity to improve your writing, but also learn to trust your instincts and make intentional choices based on your vision for your story.

Receiving feedback on your writing can be challenging, as it can feel personal and bring up feelings of sensitivity. However, it's important to approach feedback with an open mind and not take it personally. One helpful approach is to remember that feedback is an opportunity for growth and improvement. It is not indicative of your worth as a writer/author, but rather an opportunity to learn and refine your craft. Keep in mind that everyone has different perspectives and opinions, and feedback can provide valuable insights to help you see your work from different angles. Stay open, acknowledge areas for improvement, and use feedback as a tool to hone your writing skills. Having a growth mindset and not taking feedback personally, you can approach it with a more objective and constructive perspective, leading to continued growth and improvement.

Celebrate Your Achievements: Take pride in your accomplishments as an author. Celebrate each milestone, whether it's completing a chapter, finishing a draft, or getting published. Recognize your progress and the hard work you put in. Acknowledge your achievements and use them as a source of confidence in your abilities.

Overcome Self-Doubt: It's natural for self-doubt to creep in as an author. Acknowledge those feelings, but don't let them define you or your writing. Challenge negative thoughts and replace them with positive affirmations. Remind yourself of your skills, talents, and achievements. Don't forget to surround yourself with a supportive writing community that can uplift and encourage you.

Stay Persistent: Writing, for some, can be a challenging and sometimes daunting process. It's important to stay persistent and keep writing, even when self-doubt or challenges arise. Remember that writing is a skill that improves with practice, and every word you write contributes to your growth. Keep pushing forward and trust in your God-given abilities.

Share Your Writing: The ultimate test of

your confidence as an author is sharing your work with others. Be brave and share your writing with readers, whether it's through self or traditional publishing, or sharing your work with friends and family. Embrace the vulnerability of putting your writing out into the world and be proud of what you have created.

In conclusion, confidence in your writing is crucial for success as an author. Embrace your unique voice, believe in your story, embrace feedback, celebrate your achievements, overcome self-doubt, stay persistent, and share your writing with others. With confidence in your work, you can connect with readers and share your story in a powerful and impactful way. Embrace your writing with confidence and watch your author journey flourish.

Nine

Marketing Your Book

Congratulations! You've read this short book and hopefully are ready to start or continue the book writing and publishing process. Once the book is published, it will be time to share it with the world. Marketing plays a crucial role in reaching your target audience and gaining traction for your book. Here are some suggested marketing tips for authors to help you promote your book and increase its visibility:

Determine who is your target audience of readers. Before you start marketing your book, it's essential to identify your target audience. Who are the ideal readers for your book? What demographics, interests, & behaviors do they have? Understanding your target audience will help you tailor your marketing efforts to reach the right people and maximize your impact.

This is a key point, develop an Author Brand. Establishing a strong author brand is key to building your author platform and attracting readers. Create a professional author website, create social media profiles, and use consistent branding elements, such as a logo or color scheme, across your marketing materials. Your author brand should reflect your unique voice and style, helping you connect with your audience and build a loyal fan base. Please contact us, RLW Empowerment Services, LLC, info@drrobempowerment.com, if you want assistance in this area.

You must also leverage your social media. Social media platforms are powerful marketing tools for authors. Use platforms like Facebook, Instagram, Twitter, or LinkedIn to connect with readers, share updates about your book, and engage in conversations. Share valuable content, such as excerpts from your book, behind-the-scenes insights, or relevant articles to keep your audience engaged and interested.

Don't let this tip overwhelm you. But remember the first thing seen is your book cover. Therefore, creating a compelling book cover and blurb/tagline are critical elements in drawing in the readers. Invest in a professionally designed book cover that is visually appealing and conveys the essence of your book. Craft a compelling blurb that hooks readers and makes them eager to read more. These elements are often the first impression readers have of your book, so do your best to make sure they are compelling and intriguing-be true to you.

Positive book reviews can significantly

impact the success of your book. Reach out to book bloggers, online reviewers, and influencers in your genre to request reviews. Offer free copies of your book in exchange for an honest review. Positive reviews can generate buzz, increase your book's credibility, and encourage readers to give your book a try.

Hosting virtual events, such as book launches, author Q&A sessions, or online readings, are excellent ways to connect with your audience and generate interest in your book. Use platforms like Zoom or social media live streams to host virtual events and engage with your readers. Promote these events through your author website, social media, and email list to generate attendance.

Email Marketing is a building email tool for interested readers and is a valuable asset for authors. You can also consider offering a compelling lead magnet, such as a free sample chapter or exclusive content, to encourage readers to sign up for your newsletter. Use email marketing to keep your subscribers updated on your book's progress, share news and exclusive offers, and nurture relationships with your readers.

Collaborate with local and across state lines of bookstores and libraries. Local bookstores and libraries can be valuable partners in promoting your book. Reach out to local bookstores and libraries to schedule book signings, author talks, or other events. Offer to provide free copies of your book for their shelves or participate in local book fairs or festivals. Collaborating with these institutions can help you expand your reach and connect with local readers.

Another useful tool to utilize are Book Promotion Websites. There are numerous book promotion websites that cater to indie authors. Research and submit your book to reputable book promotion websites that align with your genre and target audience. These websites often offer features, author interviews, newsletter or social media promotions, which can help you reach a wider audience and generate book sales.

Most of the time there is a fee attached. Therefore, do you research to see if it is a worthwhile investment. Run limited-time promotions, such as discounted prices, free eBook downloads, or exclusive offers, can create a sense of urgency and encourage readers to a call to action.

References

https://www.sfwriters.org/27-reasons-to-write-a-book-and-how-to-finally-make-it-happen/

https://askwonder.com/research/business-books-published-worldwide-year-annual-numbers-past-ten-years-ideal-qcrwjft2o

GETTING OUT OF MY OWN WAY: Robinson, Mrs Tilesa L, Watts Jr, Dr Robert L: 9781074576837: Amazon.com: Books. (n.d.-b). https://www.amazon.com/GETTING-OUT-MY-OWN-WAY/dp/1074576837

Book Writing Exercise

You will be an author one day soon. People are going to want your autograph in their book. Use the following lines and practice your signature. Try different pen types.

Write out the theme of your book?

____

____

____

____

____

Who are the main characters (if applicable)?

____

____

____

What genre would you categorize your book?

____

____

Write your plan of action to draft the book:

____

____

____

____

____

____

About The Author

Robert Jr. has been in ministry for over 35 years and offers a refreshing perspective as he delivers his messages with a touch of humor, relevancy, and inspiration.

Robert is a native of the Chicagoland area and an ordained minister. He is the Founder and CEO of RLW Empowerment Services, LLC., which is designed to empower others through small business consulting, book publishing, and self-development  programs. Through his educational pursuits Robert holds a Doctor of Ministry, Master of Education, along with other certifications in various areas of specialties. For over a decade, he and his wife served as the Directors of the Marriage & Family Department at a mega-church in northwest Indiana. Robert has authored and published over ten books. Robert has an ardent desire to empower those who are called into ministry; therefore, he founded One Flesh Ministries Bible Institute, which offers degree programs in various ministry related subjects.

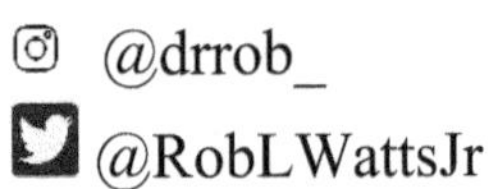
@drrob_
@RobLWattsJr

RLW EMPOWERMENT SERVICES, LLC

RLW Empowerment Services, LLC is incorporated in the State of Illinois and has a DBE certification. RLW Empowerment Services is a one-stop solution for business, personal, and spiritual development. Our comprehensive range of services includes small business consultation, full book publishing services, personal development training, Christian ministry services, as well as workshops and seminars. We are dedicated to providing you with top-notch services tailored to your unique requirements.

www.drrobempowerment.com

@mentalmotive40

@RLWEmpowerment

One Flesh Ministries Bible Institute (OFMBI) is the educational division of One Flesh Ministries, Inc. OFMBI provides Biblically-based mentorship, equip, and release those who are willing to accept the CHALLENGE of advancement and excellence in the Kingdom of God. OFMBI's goal is to provide a curriculum rooted in sound Biblical doctrine in order to achieve advancement and excellence in ministry. OFMBI is a Satellite Teaching and Testing Center (STTC) of the Institute for Christian Works, headquartered in the state of South Carolina, from which all degrees and certificates are granted. OFMBI provides quality, affordable, and 100% Independent Study Bible-based educational programs. Ministry leadership training is also available for pastors and lay leaders.

www.ofmbi.com

 @ofmbi

 @ofmbi

Author's Additional Publications

ROBERT L. WATTS, JR.
SINGLED OUT
Insights for Singles from the Gospel of Jesus

un recurso para aquellos llamados al ministerio de liderazgo
L.E.A.D.
Adoptado, nombrado y ungido
aprender del Llamado de Moisés para guiar
Robert L. Watts, Jr.
Prefacio por Pastor Peto Medina

LIVING LIFE
IN PURPOSE
ON PURPOSE
YOU WEREN'T CREATED
TO JUST EXIST
ROBERT L. WATTS, JR.

SOUL TO SOUL
MEN OF DESTINY
PURSUING GOD'S HEART
ROBERT L. WATTS, JR.